D0276927

The
NEW BATH GUIDE

Christopher Anstey

The
New Bath Guide

with an introduction by
Kenneth G. Ponting

Adams & Dart

First published in 1766
This edition © 1970 Adams & Dart
40 Gay Street, Bath, Somerset
S.B.N. 239 00075 7
Printed in Great Britain by Redwood Press Ltd,
Trowbridge and London

CHRISTOPHER ANSTEY

'What pleasure you have to come! There is a new thing published that will make you bepiss your cheeks with laughter. It is called The New Bath Guide. It stole into the world, and for a fortnight no soul looked upon it, concluding its name was its true name. No such thing. It is a set of letters in verse, in all kinds of verses describing the life of Bath, and incidentally everything else—but so much wit, so much humour, fun, poetry, so much originality, never met together before. Then the man has a better ear than Dryden or Handel. Apropos to Dryden, he has burlesqued his St. Cecilia, that you will never read it again without laughing. There is a description of a milliner's box in all the terms of landscape, *painted lawns and chequered shades*, a Moravian ode and a Moravian ditty that are incomparable, and the best names that are ever composed. I can say it by heart, though a quarto, and if I had time I would write it down for it is not yet reprinted and not one to be had'.[1]

So Horace Walpole wrote to Montague on 20 June 1766.

Christopher Anstey, the author of this most successful poem, was born at Brinkley in Cambridgeshire, where his father was Rector, on 31 October 1724. He was at school at Eton, and then went to King's College, Cambridge, where he achieved some fame for his Latin verses. He became a Fellow, but his M.A. was withheld due to lack of seriousness in his Latin orations. His son describes the position well:

'King's College had immemorially exercised the right of qualifying its members for their degree within the walls of their own society without that regular performance of acts and exercises generally in use in the university schools, and required of other colleges. It had been proposed as a salutory regulation and a first employment for the bachelor fellows of Kings that they should occasionally compose Latin declamations, and pronounce them in public school, a regulation altogether new and unprecedented in the annals of Kings College. My father, who was at that time of six years' standing in the university and the Senior Batchelor of his year, finding himself suddenly called upon to make a Latin oration upon a given subject, resisted it in common with the rest of the junior fellows as a degradation and an entrenchment on the privileges of the society. The declamation, however, was exacted and not to be dispensed with; it was accordingly made and the exordium no sooner pronounced than the orator fell suddenly into a rhapsody of adverbs so ingeniously and pointedly disposed as to convey an obvious meaning without the aid of much grammatical connections, and being delivered with great animation and emphasis, conveyed a censure and ridicule upon the whole proceedings. The orator was in consequence immediately ordered to descend from the rostrum, a circumstance to which he adverts in another declamation he was shortly afterwards called upon to make instead of the one in which he had been so unfortunately interrupted'.[2]

A second declamation brought the same approach, 'the latinity of this declamation is classical; the tenor of it exculpatory but in the highest strain of irony; the contest was carried on with the most perfect good humour on the popular side of the question, but at the same time was such a commanding and successful spirit of raillery and ridicule as could not fail to awake the resentment of the grave and reverend seniors of the university, and to produce this consequence in the following year, which were most natural to be expected from it, and which are so pathetically regretted by the author in the following lines in the appendix to the New Bath Guide:

> At Granta, sweet Granta, where studious of ease,
> Seven years did I sleep and then lost my degree.'

In 1754 he succeeded to the family estates and left Cambridge, and then in 1756 he married Ann, third daughter of Felix Culvert of Albury Hall, Herts., and sister of his oldest and most intimate friend John Calvert. Although cultivating the arts as well as his estates, Anstey published nothing for some years, but visits to Bath led, in 1766, to his most famous work—*The New Bath Guide*, or Memoirs of the B—— R—— H—— (Blunderhead) family, which so delighted Walpole. It is in many ways a remarkable work, which today can be read with far more enjoyment than many more famous and pretentious eighteenth-century poems. As Walpole pointed out, it is technically brilliant, with many changes in metre ranging from the longer lines like:

> What place, my dear Mother, with Bath can compare?
> Let Bristol for commerce and dirt be renouned,
> And Salisbury penknives and scissors to grind,

> The towns of Devizes and Bradford and Frome
> May boast that they better can manage the loom,
> I believe that they may: but the world to refine
> In manners, in dress, in politeness to shine
> Oh Bath let the art, let the glory be thine

to shorter-lined verses which are particularly good, and
this continual change of form adds considerably to the
variety, and therefore enjoyment, of the poem:

> Harken Lady Betty, harken
>   To the dismal news I tell;
> How your friends are all embarking
>   For the fiery gulf of hell.

> Brother Simkin's grown a rakehell
>   Cards and dances all the day,
> Jenny laughs at Tabernacle,
>   Tabby Runt is gone astray.

The occasional note should not be overlooked—for
example: 'The editor for many reasons begs to be excused
giving the public the sequel of this young lady's letter;
but if the reader will please to look into the Bishop of
Exeter's book entitled "The Enthusiasm of Methodists
and Paptists Compared" he will find many instances, par-
ticularly of young people who have been elected in this
manner also'.

The poem was universally praised: by Walpole, as
quoted earlier, and also notably by Gray, whose famous
Elegy in a Country Churchyard, Anstey translated into
Latin and sent to Gray. Gray suggested certain emenda-
tions and thought perhaps that in the famous lines:

> Some village Hampden that with dauntless breast
>   The little tyrant of his fields withstood,
> Some mute inglorious Milton here may rest
>   Some Cromwell guiltless of his country's blood.

the proper names should also be translated, or rather re-
placed, by appropriate Latin heroes. Anstey doubted this,
and in fact was at some pains to question the value of
what he had done. Perhaps he suspected that subtle Gray
was gently pulling his leg.

The New Bath Guide has continued to be admired, but the
tendency has been to dismiss Anstey's other work. Saints-
bury, in *The Cambridge History of English Literature*, de-
clares that he 'never achieved any other that was of even
the slightest value'. Contemporary opinion, however,
gave considerable praise to *The Election Ball, a Political*

Letter from Mr. Inkle at Bath to his Wife at Gloucester (1776) and it is certainly most readable. The poem was written after Anstey had settled in Bath and had become a member of Mrs. Miller's *coterie* at Batheaston, at that time a well-known literary salon. The subject had been suggested there and purported to be letters from an honest haberdasher and freeman of Bath giving an account of the election in the city to his wife in Gloucester.

As this poem is comparatively little known, two extracts may be of interest. First the beginning:

> And so as I told thee before my dear wife,
> I'll go to the ball tho' it costs me my life—
> Must I be shut up till like poor neighbour Snarler
> I be smok'd like a joss in my own little parlour?
> No—I'd have thee to know I can walk pretty stout
> Since I found an infallable cure for the gout,
> For the doctor I've tried has, with wedges and pegs
> So stretched out my sinews, and hammer'd my legs,
> So suppled the joint by tormenting the tendon,
> My heel I cān raise, and my toe I can bend down,
> And by Jove I'm resolved to get out of the bilboes,
> And shake at the ball both my legs and my elbows.

But to modern taste Anstey is more enjoyable in his shorter lines, where his lightness of touch and genuine sense of fun comes through best:

> To a cap like a bat
> (Which was once my cravat)
> Part gracefully platted and pin'd is,
> Part stuck upon gauze
> Resembles mackaws
> And all the fine birds of the Indies.
>
> But above all the rest
> A bold Amazon'd crest
> Waves nodding from shoulder to shoulder,
> At once to surprise
> And to ravish all eyes,
> To frighten and charm the beholder.
>
> In short, head and feather
> And wig altogether
> With wonder and joy would delight ye,
> Like the picture I've seen
> Of th' adorable queen
> Of *beautiful, blest* Otaheitee.
>
> Who gave such a ball
> To our merry men all,

And there did so frisk and dance it,
    Some thought her as fine—
    And some did opine,
'Twas VENUS herself in her TRANSIT.

    While the black maids of honour
    What waited upon her,
(The sight so uncommon and odd is)
    Brought philosopher's eyes,
    From the orbs in the skies, .
To gaze at THEIR heavenly bodies.

    But MADGE at the Rooms
    Must beware of her plumes,
For if VULCAN her feather embraces,
    Like poor Lady LAYCOCK
    She'll burn like a haycock,
And roast all the Loves and the Graces.

    How crampt in this picture
    They wriggled and tost her
While every step that they trod,
    Her foretop and nose
    Beat time to their toes,
And her feather went—niddity-nod.

Anstey does not use this form elsewhere in *An Election Ball*, which may well account for its relative dullness when compared with *The New Bath Guide*. This does suggest another and deeper criticism: the epigrammatic approach needed for the set eighteenth-century rhymed couplet was not really suited to Anstey's minor, but nevertheless, very real gift for writing light verses. If he had realised this, Anstey might well have become one of our better writers of that somewhat neglected, but delightful, verse-form which can only be described as Light Verse. It is perhaps with such masterpieces of this type as Jay's *Trivia*, Carroll, Lear and, in our own time, Eliot's *Old Possum's Book of Practical Cats* that Anstey should be compared.

However, generally speaking Anstey essentially remains a figure that is remembered in the history of English poetry because of *The New Bath Guide*.

The short Life which his son added as an introduction to the Poetical Works of 1808 gives a pleasant picture of his life in Bath:

'He rose early in the morning and was constant on horseback at his usual hour and in all seasons. His summers were uniformly spent at Cheltenham with his family, during the latter part of his life, and upon his return to Bath in the autumn he fell into the same unruffled scene of domestic ease and tranquility, rendered every day more joyous and interesting to him by the increase of his family circle and the enlargement of his hospitable table, and by many circumstances and occurrences connected with the welfare of his children which gave him infinite delight and satisfaction'.

After a remarkably happy life Anstey died in Wiltshire at the residence of his son-in-law at the age of 81.

BIBLIOGRAPHICAL NOTE

The New Bath Guide passed through many editions during the years immediately following its first publication. The *Cambridge Bibliography of English Literature* notes 1766 (Dublin), 1766, 1767, 1768 (Dublin), 1768, 1772, 1773, 1784, 1788, 1797, 1804.

There is an excellent collection of these in the Bath Reference Library, together with an un-dated edition (*c.* 1825) which was published from the Abbey Churchyard, Bath. It seems appropriate that it is this edition which is here reprinted, by kind permission of the Chief Librarian.

[1] The Yale Edition of Horace Walpole's Correspondence ed. W. S. Seers, p. 218.

[2] Introduction to the 1803 edition of Anstey's Works.

THE

NEW BATH GUIDE;

OR,

MEMOIRS

OF THE

B—N—R—D FAMILY:

IN A SERIES OF

POETICAL EPISTLES.

———◆———

By CHRISTOPHER ANSTEY, Esq.

OF TRUMPINGTON, CAMBRIDGESHIRE.

———◆———

Nullus in orbe locus Baiis prælucet amœnis.—Hor.

———

BATH: PRINTED BY M. MEYLER, ABBEY CHURCH-YARD;
AND SOLD BY ALL BOOKSELLERS.

CONTENTS.

PART THE FIRST.

PART THE SECOND.

CONTENTS.

To the Reader.

I HERE present you with a Collection of Letters, written by a
Family during their residence at Bath. The first of them, from a
romantic young Lady, addressed to her Friend in the Country, will
bring you acquainted with the rest of the Characters, and save you
the trouble of reading a dull introductory Preface from

Your humble Servant,

THE AUTHOR.

THE

NEW BATH GUIDE.

Part the First.

MISS JENNY W—d—r, TO LADY ELIZ. M—d—ss, AT
—— CASTLE, NORTH.

A View from the Parades at Bath, with some Account of the
Dramatis Personæ.

SWEET are yon' hills that crown this fertile vale!
Ye genial springs! Pierian waters, hail!

Hail, woods and lawns! Yes—oft I'll tread
   Yon' pine-clad mountain's side,
Oft trace the gay enamell'd mead,
   Where Avon rolls his pride.

Sure next to fair Castalia's streams,
   And Pindus' flow'ry path,
Apollo most the springs esteems,
   And verdant meads of *Bath*.

The Muses haunt these hallow'd groves,
   And here their vigils keep,
Here teach fond swains their hapless loves
   In gentle strains to weep.

From water sprung, like flow'rs from dew,
   What troops of bards appear?
The good of verse and physic too,
   Inspires them twice a year.

B

Take then, my friend, the sprightly rhyme,
While you, inglorious, waste your prime,
At home in cruel durance pent,
On dull domestic cares intent,
Forbid, by parents' harsh decree,
To share the joys of *Bath* with me.
Ill-judging parent! blind to merit,
Thus to confine a nymph of spirit!
With all thy talents doom'd to fade,
And wither in th' unconscious shade!
I vow, my dear, it moves my spleen,
Such frequent instances I've seen,
Of fathers, cruel and unkind,
To all paternal duty blind.
What wretches do we meet with often,
Whose hearts no tenderness can soften!
Sure all good authors should expose
Such parents, both in verse and prose;
And nymphs inspire with resolution
Ne'er to submit to persecution.
This wholesome satire much enhances
The merit of our best romances.
And modern plays that I could mention,
With judgment fraught and rare invention, }
Are writen with the same intention.
But, thank my stars! that worthy pair,
Who undertook a guardian's care,
My spirit never have confin'd ;
(An instance of their gen'rous mind ;)
For Lady B—n—r—d, my aunt,
Herself proposed this charming jaunt,
All from redundancy of care
For Sim, her fav'rite son and heir ;
To him the joyous hours I owe
That *Bath's* enchanting scenes bestow;
Thanks to her book of choice receipts,
That pamper'd him with sav'ry meats;
Nor less that day deserves a blessing,
She cramm'd his sister to excess in:
For now she sends both son and daughter,
For crudities to drink the water.
And here they are, all bile and spleen,
The strangest fish that e'er were seen

With Tabby Runt, their maid, poor creature,
The queerest animal in nature.
I'm certain none of Hogarth's sketches,
E'er form'd a set of stranger wretches.
I own, my dear, it hurts my pride,
To see them blund'ring by my side ;
My spirits flag, my life and fire
Is mortified *au désespoir*,
When Sim, unfashionable ninny,
In public calls me *Cousin Jenny*.
And yet, to give the wight his due,
He has some share of humour too,
A comic vein of pedant learning
His conversation you'll discern in,
The oddest compound you can see,
Of shrewdness and simplicity ;
With natural strokes of awkward wit,
That oft, like Parthian arrows, hit ;
For when he seems to dread the foe,
He always strikes the hardest blow ;
And when you'd think he means to flatter,
His panegyrics turn to satire :
But then no creature you can find,
Knows half so little of mankind.
Seems always blundering in the dark,
And always making some remark ;
Remarks that so provoke one's laughter,
One can't imagine what he's after :
And sure you'll thank me for exciting
In Sim a wond'rous itch for writing ;
With all his serious grimace,
To give descriptions of the place.
No doubt his mother will produce
His poetry for general use,
And if his bluntness does not fright you,
His observations must delight you ;
For truly the good creature's mind
Is honest, generous, and kind :
If unprovok'd, will ne'er displease ye,
Or ever make one soul uneasy.
I'll try to make his sister Prue
Take a small trip to Pindus too.

And Me the Nine shall all inspire
To tune for thee the warbling lyre ;
For thee the Muse shall every day
Speed, by the post, her rapid way.
For thee, my friend, I'll oft explore
Deep treasures of romantic lore :
Nor wonder if I Gods create,
As all good bards have done of late;
'Twill make my verse run smooth and even,
To call new deities from heaven :
Come then, thou Goddess I adore,
But soft—my chairman's at the door,   }
The ball's begun—my friend, no more   }
Bath, 1766.   J— W—D—R.

LETTER II.

Mr. SIMKIN B—N—R—D, to LADY B—N—R—D, AT
—— HALL, NORTH.

*Mr. B-n-r-d's Reflections on his Arrival at Bath.—The Case
of Himself and Company.—The acquaintance he com-
mences, &c. &c.*

WE all are a wonderful distance from home!
Two hundred and sixty long miles are we come!
And sure you'll rejoice, my dear mother, to hear
We are safely arriv'd at the sign of the Bear.
   'Tis a plaguy long way!—but I ne'er can repine;
As my stomach is weak and my spirits decline:
For the people say here, be whatever your case,
You are sure to get well if you come to this place,
Miss Jenny made fun, as she always is wont,
Of Prudence my sister, and Tabitha Runt;
And every moment she heard me complain,
Declar'd I was vapour'd, and laugh'd at my pain.
What tho' at Devizes I fed pretty hearty,
And made a good meal, like the rest of the party,
When I came here to Bath, not a bit could I eat,
Though the man at the Bear had provided a treat:
And so I went quite out of spirits to bed,
With wind in my stomach and noise in my head.

As we all came for health, as a body may say,
I sent for the doctor the very next day,
And the doctor was pleas'd, tho' so short was the warning,
To come to our lodging betimes in the morning;
He look'd very thoughtful and grave to be sure,
And I said to myself,—there's no hopes of a cure!
But I thought I should faint, when I saw him, dear mother,
Feel my pulse with one hand, with a watch in the other;
No token of death that is heard in the night
Could ever have put me so much in a fright;
Thinks I—'tis all over—my sentence is past,
And now he is counting how long I may last.
Then he look'd at ——, and his face grew so long,
I'm sure he thought something within me was wrong.
He determin'd our cases, at length (God preserve us!)
I'm bilious, I find, and the women are nervous;
Their systems relax'd, and all turn'd topsy-turvy,
With hypochondriacs, obstructions, and scurvy,
And these are distempers he must know the whole on,
For he talk'd of the peritonœum and colon,
Of phlegmatic humours oppressing the women,
From feculent matter that swells the abdomen;
But the noise I have heard in my bowels like thunder,
Is a flatus, I find, in my left hypochonder,
So plenty of med'cines each day does he send ⎫
Post singulas liquidas sedes sumend'   ⎬
Ad crepitus vesper' & man' promovend' ;   ⎭
In English to say, we must swallow a potion,
For driving out wind after every motion;
The same to continue for three weeks at least,
Before we may venture the waters to taste.
Five times have I purg'd, yet I'm sorry to tell ye,
I find the same gnawing and wind in my belly;
But, without any doubt, I shall find myself stronger,
When I've took the same physic a week or two longer.
He gives little Tabby a great many doses,
For he says the poor creature has got the *Chlorosis*,
Or a ravenous *Pica*, so brought on the vapours
By swallowing stuff she had read in the papers;
And often I marvell'd she spent so much money
In *Water-dock Essence* and *Balsam of Honey* ;
Such tinctures, elixirs, such pills have I seen,
I never could wonder her face was so green.

Yet he thinks he can very soon set her to right
With *Testic' Equin'* that she takes ev'ry night;
And when to her spirits and strength he has brought her,
He thinks she may venture to bathe in the water.
But Prudence is forc'd ev'ry day to ride out,
For he says she wants thoroughly jumbling about.
Now it happens in this very house is a lodger,
Whose name's Nicodemus, but some call him Roger;
And Roger's so kind as my sister to bump
On a pillion, as soon as she comes from the pump;
He's a pious good man and an excellent scholar,
And I think it is certain no harm can befall her;
For Roger is constantly saying his prayers,
Or singing some spiritual hymn on the stairs.
But my cousin Miss Jenny's as fresh as a rose,
And the Captain attends her wherever she goes:
The Captain's a *worthy good sort of a man*,
For he calls in upon us whenever he can,
And often a dinner or supper he takes here,
And Jenny and he talk of Milton and Shakespeare,
For the life of me, now, I cant think of his name,
But we all got acquainted as soon as we came.

Don't wonder, dear mother, in verse I have writ,
For Jenny declares I've a good pretty wit;
She says that she frequently sends a few verses
To friends and acquaintance, and often rehearses;
Declares 'tis the fashion, and all the world knows
There's nothing so filthy so vulgar as prose.
And I hope, as I write without any connection,
I shall make a great figure in Dodsley's Collection;
At least, when he chooses his book to increase,
I may take a small flight as a *fugitive piece*.
But now, my dear mother, I'm quite at a stand,
So I rest your dutiful son to command.

   Bath, 1766.   S. B—N—R—D.

LETTER III.

Miss Jenny W—d—r, to Lady Eliz. M—d—ss,
        at —— Castle, North.

The Birth of Fashion: a Specimen of a Modern Ode.

Sure there are charms by Heaven assigned
    To modish life alone;
A grace, an air, a taste refin'd,
    To vulgar souls unknown.

Nature, my friend, profuse in vain,
    May every gift impart;
If unimprov'd, she ne'er can gain
    An empire o'er the heart.

Dress be our care in this gay scene
    Of Pleasure's best abode:
Enchanting Dress! if well I ween,
    Meet subject for an Ode.

Come then, nymph of various mien,
Votary true of Beauty's Queen,
Whom the young and aged adore,
And thy different arts explore:
Fashion come:—on me a while
Deign, fantastic nymph, to smile.
Moria* thee, in times of yore,
To the motley Proteus bore:
He, in Bishop's robes array'd,
Went one night to masquerade,
Where thy simple mother strayed:
She was clad like harmless quaker,
And was pleased my Lord should take her
By the waist and kindly shake her;
And with look demure, said she,
" Pray, my Lord—*do you know me?*"
He, with soothing, flattering arts,
Such as win all female hearts,

* The Goddess of Folly.

Much extoll'd her wit and beauty,
And declar'd it was his duty,
As she was a maid of honour,
To confer his blessing on her.
There, 'mid dress of various hue,
Crimson, yellow, green, and blue,
All on furbelows and laces,
Slipt into her chaste embraces;
Then, like a sainted rogue, cried he,
" Little Quaker—*you know me.*"

   Fill'd with thee she went to *France*,
Land renown'd for complaisance,
Versed in science debonair,
Bowing, dancing, dressing hair;
There she chose her habitation,
Fix'd thy place of education.
Nymph, at thy auspicious birth,
Hebe strew'd with flowers the earth;
Thee to welcome, all the Graces
Deck'd in ruffles, deck'd in laces,
With the God of Love attended,
And the Cyprian Queen descended.
Now you trip it o'er the globe,
Clad in party-coloured robe,
And with all thy mother's sense,
Virtues of your sire dispense.

   Goddess, if from hand like mine, $\Big\}$
Aught be worthy of thy shrine,
Take the flow'ry wreath I twine.
Lead, oh! lead me by the hand,
Guide me with thy magic wand,
Whether decked in lace and ribbons,
Thou appear'st like Mrs. Gibbons,
Or the nymph of smiling look,
At *Bath* yclept Janetta Cook.
Bring, O bring thy essence-pot,
Amber, musk, and bergamot,
Eau de chipre, eau de luce,
Sans pareil, and citron juice,
Nor thy band-box leave behind,
Fill'd with stores of every kind;
All th' enraptur'd bard supposes,
Who to Fancy odes composes;

All that Fancy's self has feign'd,
In a band-box is contained:
Painted lawns, and chequer'd shades, }
Crape that's worn by love-lorn maids, }
Water'd tabbies, flower'd brocades;   }
Vi'lets, pinks, Italian posies,
Myrtles, jessamins, and roses,
Aprons, caps, and 'kerchiefs clean,
Straw-built hats and bonnets green,
Catguts, gauzes, tippets, ruffs,
Fans, and hoods, and feather'd muffs,
Stomachers, and Paris-nets,   }
Ear-rings, necklaces, aigrets,   }
Fringes, blonds, and mignionets;   }
Fine vermillion for the cheek,
Velvet patches *à la Grecque.*
Come, but don't forget the gloves,
Which, with all the smiling loves,
Venus caught young Cupid picking
From the tender breast of chicken;
Little chicken, worthier far
Than the birds of Juno's car,
Soft as Cytherea's dove,
Let thy skin my skin improve;
Thou by night shall grace my arm,
And by day shall teach to charm.
   Then, O sweet Goddess, bring with thee
Thy boon attendant Gaiety,
Laughter, Freedom, Mirth, and Ease,
And all the smiling deities;
Fancy spreading painted sails,
Loves that fan with gentle gales.
But hark!—methinks I hear a voice,
My organs all at once rejoice;
A voice that *says,* or *seems to say,* }
" Sister, hasten, sister gay,   }
" Come to the pump-room—come away."   }

Bath, 1766.   J—— W—D—R.

LETTER IV.

MR. SIMKIN B—N—R—D, to LADY B—N—R—D, AT
——HALL, NORTH.

A Consultation of Physicians.

DEAR mother, my time has been wretchedly spent,
With a gripe or a hiccup wherever I went;
My stomach all swell'd till I thought it would burst;
Sure never poor mortal with wind was so curst!
If ever I ate a good supper at night,
I dream'd of the devil, and wak'd in a fright:
And so, as I grew every day worse and worse,
The doctor advised me to send for a nurse;
And the nurse was so willing my health to restore,
She begg'd me to send for a few doctors more;
For when any difficult work's to be done,
Many heads can dispatch it much better than one;
And I find there are doctors enough at this place,
If you want to consult on a dangerous case!
So they all met together, and thus began talking.—
" Good doctor, I'm your's—'tis a fine day for walking—
" Sad news in the papers—God knows who's to blame!
" The Colonies seem to be all in a flame;
" This *Stamp Act*, no doubt, might be good for the Crown,
" But I fear 'tis a pill that will never go down—
" What can *Portugal* mean? Is *she* going to stir up
" Convulsions and heats in the bowels of *Europe?*
" Twill be fatal if *England* relapses again,
" From the ill blood and humours of *Bourbon* and *Spain.*"
Says I, " my good doctors, I can't understand,
" Why the deuce you take so many patients in hand;
" You've a great deal of practice, so far as I find,
" But since you're come hither, do pray be so kind, }
" To write me down something that's good for the wind. }
" No doubt ye are all of ye great politicians,
" But at present my bowels have need of physicians;
" Consider my case in the light it deserves,
" And pity the state of my stomach and nerves."
But a tight little doctor began to dispute
About administrations, Newcastle, and Bute;
Talk'd much of economy, much of profuseness.
Says another, "This case, which at first was a looseness,

" Is become a *Tenesmus*, and all we can do
" Is to give him a gentle cathartic or two;
" First get off the phlegm that adheres to the *plicœ*,
" Then throw in a med'cine that's pretty and spicy;
" A *peppermint* draught, or a—Come, let's begone,
" We've another bad case to consider at one."
So thus they brush'd off, each his cane at his nose,
When Jenny came in, who had heard all their prose;
" I'll teach them," said she, " at their next consultation,
" To come and take fees for the good of the nation."
I could not conceive what the devil she meant,
But she seiz'd all the stuff that the doctor had sent,
And out of the window she flung it down souse,
As the first politician went out of the house.
Decoctions and syrups around him all flew,
The pill, bolus, julep, and apozem too;
His wig had the luck a cathartic to meet,
And squash went the gallipot under his feet.
She said, 'twas a shame I should swallow such stuff,
When my bowels were weak, and the physic so rough;
Declar'd she was shock'd that so many should come
To be doctor'd to death such a distance from home,
At a place where they tell you that water alone,
Can cure all distempers that ever were known.
But, what is the pleasantest part of the story,
She has ordered for dinner a piper and dory:
For to-day Captain Cormorant's coming to dine,
That worthy acquaintance of Jenny's and mine.
'Tis a shame to the army that men of such spirit,
Should never obtain the reward of their merit;
For the Captain's as gallant a man, I'll be sworn,
And as honest a fellow as ever was born:
After so many hardships and dangers incurr'd,
He himself thinks he ought to be better preferr'd;
And Roger, or what is his name ? Nicodemus,
Appears full as kind, and as much to esteem us.
Our Prudence declares he's an excellent preacher,
And by night and by day he's so good as to teach her;
His doctrine so sound with such spirit he gives,
She ne'er can forget it as long as she lives.
I told you before that he's often so kind,
To go out a riding with Prudence behind,

So frequently dines here without any pressing,
And now to the fish he is giving his blessing,
And as that is the case, though I've taken a griper,
I'll venture to peck at the dory and piper.
And now, my dear mother, &c. &c. &c.
  Bath, 1766.   S—— B—N—R—D.

············

LETTER V.

Mr. Simkin B—N—R—D, to Lady B—N—R—D, at
—— Hall, North.

*Salutations of Bath, and an Adventure of Mr. B—n—r—d's
    in consequence thereof.*

No city, dear mother, this city excels,
In charming sweet sounds both of fiddles and bells;
I thought like a fool, that they only would ring
For a wedding, or judge, or the birth of a king;
But I found 'twas for *me*, that the good-natur'd people
Rung so hard that I thought they would pull down the
        steeple;
So I took out my purse, as I hate to be shabby,
And paid all the men when they came from the Abbey;
Yet some think it strange they should make such a riot
In a place where sick folk would be glad to be quiet;
But I hear 'tis the business of this corporation
To welcome in all the *great* men of the nation:
For you know there is nothing diverts or employs
The minds of great people like making a noise:
So with bells they contrive all as much as they can
To tell the arrival of any such man.
If a broker or statesman, a gamester or peer,
A nat'ralized Jew, or a Bishop comes here,
Or *an eminent trader in cheese* should retire,
Just to think of the business the state may require,
With horns and with trumpets, with fiddles and drums,
They'll strive to divert him as soon as he comes;
'Tis amazing they find such a number of ways
Of employing his thoughts all the time that he stays!
If by chance the *great* man at his lodging alone is,
He may view from his window the colliers' ponies

On both the Parades, where they tumble and kick,
To the great entertainment of those that are sick:
What a number of turnspits and builders he'll find
For relaxing his cares and unbending his mind,
While notes of sweet music contend with the cries
Of *fine potted laver, fresh oysters and pies !*
And music's a thing I shall truly revere,
Since the city musicians so tickle my ear :
For when we arriv'd at Bath t' other day,
They came to our lodgings on purpose to play;
And I thought it was right, as the music was come,
To foot it a little in Tabitha's room;
For practice makes perfect, as often I've read,
And to heels is of service as well as the head;
But the lodgers were shock'd such a noise we should make,
And the ladies declar'd that we kept them awake;
Lord Ringbone who lay in the parlour below,
On account of the gout he had got in his toe,
Began on a sudden to curse and to swear:
I protest, my dear mother, 'twas shocking to hear }
The oaths of that reprobate gouty old peer:
" All the devils in hell sure at once have concurr'd
To make such a noise here as never was heard ;
Some blundering blockhead, while I am in bed,
Treads as hard as a coach-horse just over my head;
I cannot conceive what a plague he's about:
Are the fiddlers come hither to make all this rout }
With their damn'd squeaking catgut that's worse than
        the gout?
If the Aldermen bade 'em come hither, I swear,
I wish they were broiling in hell with the May'r ;
May flames be my portion if ever I give
Those rascals one farthing as long as I live!"
So while they were playing their musical airs,
And I was just dancing the hay round the chairs, }
He roar'd to his Frenchman to kick them down stairs.
The Frenchman came forth with his outlandish lingo,
Just the same as a monkey, and made all the men go;
I could not make out what he said, not a word,
And his Lordship declar'd I was very absurd.
Says I, ' Master Ringbone, I've nothing to fear,
Though you be a Lord, and your man a Mounseer, }
For the May'r and the Aldermen bade them come here :

'—— As absurd as I am,
I don't care a damn
For you nor your *valet de sham:*
For a Lord, do you see,
Is nothing to me,
Any more than a flea;
And your Frenchman so eager,
With all his soup meagre,
Is no more than a mouse,
Or a bug or a louse,
And I'll do as I please while I stay in the house:
For the B——n——r——d family all can afford
To part with their money as free as a Lord.'
    So I thank'd the musicians, and gave them a guinea,
Though the ladies and gentlemen call'd me a ninny;
And I'll give them another the next time they play, ⎫
For men of good fortune encourage, they say,   ⎬
All arts and all sciences too in their way;   ⎭
„So the men were so kind as to halloo and bawl,   ⎫
" God bless you, Sir, thank you, good fortune befall ⎬
Yourself and the B——n——r——d family all."   ⎭
    Excuse any more,—for I very well know,
Both my subject and verse—*are exceedingly low:*
But if any great critic finds fault with my letter,
He has nothing to do but to send you a better.
And now my dear mother, &c. &c. &c.
    Bath, 1766.   S—— B—N—R—D.

LETTER VI.

MR. SIMKIN B—N—R—D, TO LADY B—N—R—D, AT
—— HALL, NORTH.

Mr. B-n-r-d gives a Description of the Bathing.

THIS morning, dear mother, as soon as 'twas light,
I was wak'd by a noise that astonish'd me quite;
For in Tabitha's chamber I heard such a clatter,
I could not conceive what the deuce was the matter;
And, would you believe it, I went up and found her
In a blanket, with two lusty fellows around her,
Who both seem'd a going to carry her off in
A little black box just the size of a coffin.

' Pray tell me,' says I, ' what ye 're doing of there?'
"Why, master, 'tis hard to be bilk'd of our fare,
And so we were thrusting her into a chair;
We don't see no reason for using us so,
For she had us come hither, and now she wont go:
We've earn'd all the fare, for we both came and knock'd
        her
Up, as soon as 'twas light, by advice of the Doctor;
And this is a job that we often go a'ter,
For ladies that choose to go into the water."
' But, pray,' says I, ' Tabitha, what is your drift
To be cover'd in flannel instead of a shift?
'Tis all by the Doctor's advice, I suppose,
That nothing is left to be seen but your nose:
I think, if you really intend to go in,
'Twould do you more good if you stript to the skin;
And if you 've a mind for a frolic, i'faith,
I'll just step and see you jump into the bath.'
So they hoisted her down just as safe and as well
And as snug as a hodmandod rides in his shell;
I fain would have gone to see Tabitha dip,
But they turn'd at a corner, and gave me the slip,
Yet in searching about I had better success,
For I got to a place where the ladies undress:
Thinks I to myself, they are after some fun,
And I'll see what they 're doing, as sure as a gun:
So I peep'd at the door, and I saw a great mat
That cover'd the table, and got under that,
And laid myself down there as snug and as still,
(As a body may say) like a thief in a mill:
And of all the fine sights I have seen, my dear mother,
I never expect to behold such another:
How the ladies did giggle and set up their clacks,
All the while an old woman was rubbing their backs!
Oh 'twas pretty to see them all put on their flannels,
And then take the water like so many spaniels;
And though all the while it grew hotter and hotter,
They swam, just as if they were hunting an otter.
'Twas a glorious sight to behold the fair sex
All wading with gentlemen up to their necks,
And view them so prettily tumble and sprawl
In a great smoking kettle as big as our hall:

And to day, many persons of rank and condition
Were boil'd by command of an able physician:
Dean Spavin, Dean Mangey, and Doctor De'Squirt,
Were all sent from Cambridge to rub off their dirt;
Judge Bane, and the worthy old Counsellor Pest,
Join'd issue at once, and went in with the rest;
And this they all said was exceedingly good
For strength'ning the spirits and mending the blood,
It pleased me to see how they all were inclin'd
To lengthen their lives for the good of mankind;
For I ne'er would believe that a bishop or judge
Can fancy old Satan may owe him a grudge;
Though some think the lawyer may choose to *demur*,
And the priest till another accasion *defer:*
And both, to be better prepared for herea'ter,
Take a smack of the brimstone contain'd in the water.
But, what is surprising, no mortal e'er view'd
Any one of the physical gentlemen stew'd;
Since the day that King Bladud* first found out these
          bogs,
And thought them so good for himself and his hogs,
Not one of the Faculty ever has tried
These excellent waters to cure his own hide;
Though many a skilful and learned physician,
With candour, good sense, and profound erudition,
Obliges the world with the fruits of his brain,
Their nature and hidden effects to explain.
Thus Chiron advised Madam Thetis to take
And dip her poor child in the Stygian lake;
But the worthy old doctor was not such an elf
As ever to venture his carcase himself.
So Jason's good wife used to set on a pot,
And put in at once all the patients she'd got,
But thought it sufficient to give her direction,
Without being coddled to mend her complexion:
And I never have heard that she wrote any treatise,
To tell what the virtue of water and heat is.
You cannot conceive what a number of ladies
Were wash'd in the water the same as our maid is:
Old Baron Vanteazer, a man of great wealth,
Brought his Lady, the Baroness, here for her health;

* Vide Old Bath Guide.

The Baroness bathes, and she says that her case
Has been hit to a hair, and is mending apace:
And this is a point all the learned agree on,
The Baron has met with the fate of Acteon;
Who, while he peep'd into the bath, had the luck,
To find himself suddenly chang'd to a buck.
Miss Scratchit went in, and the Countess of Scales,
Both ladies of very great fashion in Wales;
Then all on a sudden two ladies of worth,
My Lady Pandora Macscurvy came forth,
With General Sulpher, arrived from the North.
So Tabby, you see, had the honour of washing
With folks of distinction, and very high fashion;
But in spite of good company, poor little soul,
She shook both her ears like a mouse in a bowl.

Ods-bobs! how delighted I was unawares,
With the fiddles I heard in the room above stairs;
For music is wholesome, the doctors all think,
For ladies that bathe, and for ladies that drink:
And that's the opinion of Robin our driver,
Who whistles his nags while they stand at the river:
They say it is right that for every glass
A tune you should take that the water may pass.
So while little Tabby was washing her rump,
The ladies kept drinking it out of the pump.

I've a deal more to say, but am loth to intrude
On your time, my dear mother, so now I'll conclude.
Bath, 1766.   S—— B——N——R——D.

....

LETTER VII.

MR. SIMKIN B——N——R——D, TO LADY B——N——R——D, AT
—— CASTLE, NORTH.

A Panegyric on Bath, and a Moravian Hymn.

OF all the gay places the world can afford,
By gentle and simple for pastime ador'd,
Fine balls and fine concerts, fine buildings and springs,
Fine walks and fine views, and a thousand fine things,
(Not to mention the sweet situation and air,)
What place, my dear mother, with Bath can compare?

C

Let Bristol for commerce and dirt be renown'd;
At Salisbury, penknives and scissars be ground;
The towns of Devizes, of Bradford, and Frome,
May boast that they better can manage the loom;
I believe that they may;—but the world to refine,
In manners, in dress, in politeness to shine,
Oh Bath! let the art, let the glory be thine.
I'm sure that I've travell'd our country all o'er,
And ne'er was so civilly treated before:
Would you think, my dear mother, (without the least hint
That we all should be glad of appearing in print),
The news-writers here were so kind as to give all
The world an account of our happy arrival!—
You scarce can imagine what numbers I've met,
'Though to me are they perfectly strangers as yet)
Who all with address and civility came,
And seem'd vastly proud of SUBSCRIBING our name.
Young Timothy Canvass is charm'd with the place!
Who, I hear, is come hither his fibres to brace!
Poor man! at th' Election he threw t' other day,
All his victuals, and liquor, and money away;
And some people think with such haste he began,
That soon he the constable greatly outran,
And is qualified now for a Parliament-man:
Goes every day to the coffee-house, where
The wits and the great politicians repair:
Harangues on the funds, and the state of the nation,
And plans a good speech for an Administration,
In hopes of a place, which he thinks he deserves,
As the love of his country has ruin'd his nerves.—
Our neighbour, Sir Easterlin Widgeon, has swore
He ne'er will return to his bogs any more;
The Thicksculls are settled; we've had invitations
With a great many more on the score of relations:
The Loungers are come too: old Stucco has just sent
His plan for a house to be built in the Crescent;
'Twill soon be complete, and they say all their work
Is as strong as St. Paul's, or the minster at York.
Don't you think 'twould be better to lease our estate,
And buy a good house here before 'tis too late?—
You never can go, my dear mother, where you
So much have to see, and so little to do.

I write this in haste, for the Captain is come,
And so kind as to go with us all to the room ;
But be sure by the very next post you shall hear
Of all I've the pleasure of meeting with there ;
For I scribble my verse with a great deal of ease,
And can send you a letter whenever I please ;
And while at this place I've the honour to stay,
I think I can never want something to say.
But now, my dear mother, &c. &c. &c.
  Bath, 1766.   S—— B—N—R—D.

POSTSCRIPT.

I'm sorry to find at the city of Bath
Many folks are uneasy concerning their faith .
Nicodemus, the preacher, strives all he can do
To quiet the conscience of good sister Prue ;
But Tabby from scruples of mind is releas'd,
Since she met with a learned Moravian priest,
Who says, *There is neither transgression nor sin ;*
A doctrine which brings many customers in.
She thinks this the prettiest Ode upon the earth,
Which he made on his infant that died in the birth :

ODE.*

Chicken blessed
And caressed,
Little bee on JESU's breast !
From the hurry
Of the earth thou'rt now at rest.

LETTER VIII.

MR. SIMKIN B—N—R—D, TO LADY B—N—R—D, AT
—— HALL, NORTH.

Mr. B-n-r-d goes to the Rooms ;—His Opinion of Gaming.

FROM the earliest ages, dear mother, till now,
All statesmen and great politicians allow,
That nothing advances the good of a nation,
Like giving all money a free circulation :

 * The learned Moravian has pirated this Ode from Count Zinzen-
dorf's Book of Hymns. Vide H. 33.
         C 2

This question from Members of Parliament draws
Many speeches that meet universal applause;
And if ever, dear mother, I live to be one,
I'll speak on this subject as sure as a gun:
For *Bath* will I speak, and I'll make an oration
Shall obtain me the freedom of this corporation.
I have no kind of doubt but the Speaker will beg
All the Members to *hear* when I set out my leg.
" Circulation of cash—circulation decay'd—
Is at once the destruction and ruin of trade;
Circulation—I say—circulation it is,
Gives life to commercial countries like this:"
What thanks to the city of *Bath* then are due
From all who this patriot maxim pursue!
For in no place whatever that national good
Is practis'd so well, and so well understood.
What infinite merit and praise does she claim in
Her ways and her means for promoting of *gaming!*
And *gaming*, no doubt, is of infinite use
That same circulation of cash to produce.
What true public spirited people are here,
Who for that very purpose come every year!
All eminent men, who no trade ever knew
But *gaming*, the only good trade to pursue:
All other professions are subject to fail,
But *gaming's* a business will ever prevail;
Besides 't is the only good way to commence
An acquaintance with all men of spirit and sense;
We may grub on without it through life, I suppose,
But then 'tis with people—*that nobody knows ;*
We ne'er can expect to be rich wise or great,
Or look'd upon fit for employments of state:
'Tis your men of fine heads, and of nice calculations,
That afford so much service to Administrations,
Who by frequent experience know how to devise
The speediest method of raising supplies:
'Tis such men as these, men of honor and worth,
That challenge respect from all persons of birth;
And is it not right they should all be carest,
When they're all so polite, and so very well drest,
When they circulate freely the money they've won,
And wear a lac'd coat, though their fathers wore none!

Our trade is encourag'd as much, if not more,
By the tender soft sex I shall ever adore;
But their husbands, those brutes, have been known to
      complain,
And swear they will never set foot here again.—
Ye wretches ingrate! to find fault with your wives,
The comfort, the solace, the joy of your lives!
Oh! that women, whose price is so far above rubies,
Should fall to the lot of such ignorant boobies!
Does n't Solomon speak of such women with rapture,
In verse his eleventh and thirty-first chapter?
And surely that wise king of Israel knew
What belong'd to a woman much better than you;
He says, " if you find out a virtuous wife,
She will do a man good all the days of her life;
She deals like a merchant, she sitteth up late;"
And you'll find it is written in verse twenty-eight }
" Her husband is sure to be known at the gate.
He never hath need or occasion for spoil,
When his wife is much better employed all the while;
She seeketh fine wool and fine linen she buys,
And is clothed in purple and scarlet likewise."
Now pray don't your wives do the very same thing,
And follow th' advice of that worthy old king?
Do they spare for expenses themselves in adorning?
Don't they go about buying fine things all the morning?
And at cards all the night take the trouble to play,
To get back the money they spent in the day?
And sure there's no sort of occasion to show
Ye are known at the gate, or wherever ye go.
Pray are not your ladies at Bath better plac'd }
Than the wife of a king who herself so disgrac'd,
And at Ithaca lived in *such very bad taste?*
Poor soul! while her husband thought proper to leave her,
She slaved all the day like a Spitalfields weaver,
And then, like a fool, when her web was half spun,
Pull'd to pieces at night all the work she had done.
But these to their husbands more profit can yield,
And are much like a lily that grows in the field:
They toil not indeed, nor indeed do they spin,
Yet they never are idle when once they begin,
But are very intent on increasing their store,
And always keep shuffling and cutting for more:

Industrious creatures! that make it a rule
To secure half the fish, while they *manage* the pool;
So they win, to be sure; but I very much wonder
Why they put so much money the candlestick under;
For up comes a man on a sudden, splash-dash,
Snuffs the candles, and carries away all the cash:
And as nobody troubles their heads any more,
I'm in very great hopes that it goes to the poor.—
Methinks I should like to excel in a trade
By which such a number their fortunes have made.
I've heard of a wise, philosophical Jew
That shuffles the cards in a manner that's new;
One Jonas, I think:—and could wish for the future
To have that illustrious sage for my tutor;
And the Captain, whose kindness I ne'er can forget,
Will teach me a game he calls *Lansquenet*,
So I soon shall acquaint you what money I've won;
In the mean time I rest your most dutiful son,

    Bath, 1766.   S—— B—N—R—D.

END OF THE FIRST PART.

Part the Second.

LETTER IX.

Miss Jenny W—d—r, to Lady Eliz. M—d—ss,
at —— Castle, North.

A JOURNAL.

To humbler strains, ye Nine, descend,
And greet my poor sequester'd friend.
Not odes, with rapid eagle flight,
That soar above all human sight,
Not fancy's fair and fertile field
To all the same delight can yield.
But come, Calliope, and say
How pleasure wastes the various day:
Whether thou art wont to rove
By Parade or Orange Grove,
Or to breathe a purer air
In the Circus or the Square;
Wheresoever be thy path,
Tell, O tell the joys of Bath!
 Ev'ry morning, ev'ry night,
Gayest scenes of fresh delight!
When Aurora sheds her beams,
Wak'd from soft Elysian dreams,
Music calls me to the spring,
Which can health and spirits bring:
There Hygeia, Goddess, pours
Blessings from her various stores:
Let me to her altars haste,
Though I ne'er the waters taste,
Near the pump to take my stand,
With a nosegay in my hand,

And to hear the Captain say,
" How do ye do, dear Miss, to-day?"
The Captain!—Now you'll say, my dear,
Methinks I long his name to hear.—
Why then, but don't you tell my aunt,
The Captain's name is Cormorant:
But hereafter, you must know,
I shall call him Romeo,
And your friend, dear Lady Bet,
Jenny no more, but Juliet.

O ye guardian spirits fair,
All who make true love your care,
May I oft my Romeo meet,
Oft enjoy his converse sweet;
I alone his thoughts employ,
Through each various scene of joy!
Lo! where all the jocund throng
From the Pump-room hastes along,
To the breakfast all invited
By Sir Toby, lately knighted.
See with joy my Romeo comes!
He conducts me to the Rooms;
There he whispers, not unseen,
Tender tales behind the screen;
While his eyes are fixed on mine,
See each nymph with envy pine,
And with looks of forced disdain,
Smile contempt, but sigh in vain!

O the charming parties made!
Some to walk the South-Parade,
Some to Lincomb's shady groves,
Or to Simpson's proud alcoves;
Some for Chapel trip away.
Then take places for the Play;
Or we walk about in pattens,
Buying gauzes, cheap'ning satins:
Or to Painter's we repair,
Meet Sir Peregine Hatchet there,
Pleas'd the artist's skill to trace
In his dear Miss Gorgon's face:
Happy pair! who fix'd as fate   ⎫
For the sweet connubial state,   ⎬
Smile in canvas *tete-a-tete*.   ⎭

If the weather, cold and chill,
Calls us all to Mr. Gill,
Romeo hands to me the jelly,
Or the soup of vermicelli;
If at Toyshop I step in,
He presents a diamond pin;
Sweetest token I can wear,
Which at once may grace my hair,
And, in witness of my flame,
Teach the glass to bear his name:
See him turn each trinket over,
If for me he can discover
Aught his passion to reveal,
Emblematic ring or seal;
Cupid whetting pointed darts,
For a pair of tender hearts;
Hymen lighting sacred fires,
Types of chaste and fond desires.
Thus enjoy we ev'ry blessing,
Till the toilet calls to dressing;
Where's my garnet, cap, and sprig?
Send for Singe to dress my wig:
Bring my silver'd mazarine,
Sweetest gown that e'er was seen:
Tabitha, put on my ruff:
Where's my dear delightful muff?
Muff, my faithful Romeo's present!
Tippet too from tail of pheasant!
Muff from downy breast of swan!
O the dear enchanting man!
Muff that makes me think how Jove
Flew to Leda from above—
Muff that—Tabby, see who rapt then,
" Madam, Madam, 'tis the Captain!"
Sure his voice I hear below,
'Tis, it is my Romeo!
Shape and gait, and careless air, ⎱
Diamond ring, and solitaire, ⎰
Birth and fashion all declare.
How his eyes, that gently roll,
Speak the language of his soul!
See the dimple on his cheek,
See him smile and sweetly speak;

"Lovely nymph, at your command,
"I have something in my hand,
"Which I hope you'll not refuse,
"'Twill us both this night amuse:
"What tho' Lady Whisker crave it,
"And Miss Badger long to have it,
"'Tis, by Jupiter I swear,
"'Tis for you alone, my dear:
"See this ticket, gentle maid,
"At your feet an offering laid:
"Thee the Loves and Graces call,
"To a little private ball :
"And to play I bid adieu,
"Hazard, lansquenet, and loo,
"Fairest nymph, to dance with you."
I with joy accept his ticket,
And upon my bosom stick it:
Well I know how Romeo dances,
With what air he first advances ;
With what grace his gloves he draws on,
Claps, and calls up *Nancy Dawson* :
Me thro' ev'ry dance conducting,
And the music oft instructing ;
See him tap, the time to show,
With his " light fantastic toe;"
Skill'd in ev'ry art to please,
From the fan to waft the breeze,
Or his bottle to produce,
Filled with pungent *Eau de Luce.*
Wonder not, my friend, I go
To the ball with Romeo.
    Such delights if thou canst give,
Bath, at thee I choose to live.

Bath, 1766.   J—— W—D—R.

POSTCRIPT.

Inclos'd you'll find some lines, my dear,
Made by a hungry poet here,
A happy bard who rhymes and eats,
And lives by uttering quaint conceits ;
Yet thinks to him alone belong
The laurels due to modern song.

SONG.

A CHARGE TO THE POETS.

Written at Mr. Gill's, an eminent Cook at Bath.

YE bards who sing the hero's praise,
　　Or lass's of the mill,   [*Forte.*
A loftier theme invites your lays,
　　Come tune your lyres to Gill.

Of all the cooks the world can boast,
　　However great their skill,
To bake or fry, to boil or roast,
　　There's none like Master Gill.

Sweet rhyming troop, no longer stoop
　　To drink Castalia's rill,
Whene'er ye droop, O taste the soup
　　That's made by Master Gill.

O taste this soup, for which the fair,
　　When hungry, cold, and chill,
Forsake the Circus and the Square,
　　To eat with Master Gill.

'Tis this that makes my Chloe's lips
　　Ambrosial sweets distil;   [*Affetuose.*
For leeks and cabbage oft she sips
　　In soup that's made by Gill.

Immortal bards, view here your wit,
　　The labours of your quill,
To singe the fowl upon the spit,
　　Condemned by Master Gill.

My humble verse that fate will meet,
　　Nor shall I take it ill ;
But grant, ye Gods! that I may eat
　　That fowl when drest by Gill.

These are your true poetic fires,
　　That drest this sav'ry grill;
E'en while I eat, the Muse inspires,
　　And tunes my voice to Gill.

When C——— strikes the vocal lyre,
  Sweet Lydian measures thrill;
But I the gridir'n more admire,
  When tun'd by Master Gill.

"Come take my sage of antient use,"
  Cries learned Doctor H—ll;
"But what's the sage without the goose,"
  Replies my Master Gill.

He who would fortify his mind,
  His belly first should fill;   [*Forte.*
Roast beef 'gainst terrors best you'll find;
  "*The Greeks knew this,*" says Gill.

Your spirits and your blood to stir,
  Old Galen gives a pill;
But I the forc'd meat ball prefer,
  Prepar'd by Master Gill.

While he so well can broil and bake,
  I'll promise and fulfil,
No other physic e'er to take
  Than what's prescrib'd by Gill.

Your bard has liv'd at Bath so long,   [*Piano.*
  He dreads to see your bill—
Instead of cash accept this song,   [*Pianissimo.*
  My worthy Master Gill.

....

LETTER X.

MR. SIMKIN B—N—R—D, TO LADY B—N—R—D, AT
——HALL, NORTH.

Taste and Spirit.—Mr. B-n-r-d. commences a Beau Garçon.

So lively, so gay, my dear mother I'm grown,
I do long to do something to make myself known;
For persons of taste and true spirit I find,
Are fond of attracting the eyes of mankind:
What numbers one sees, for that very reason,
Come to make such a figure at Bath every season!

'Tis this that provokes Mrs. Shenkin Ap Leek
To dine at the ord'nary twice in a week,
Though at home she might eat a good dinner in comfort,
Nor pay such a cursed extravagant sum for't :
But then her acquaintance would never have known
Mrs. Shenkin Ap Leek had acquired the *bon ton ;*
Ne'er shewn how in taste the Ap Leeks can excel
The Duchess of Truffles, and Lady Mo ell ;
Had ne'er been ador'd by Sir Pye Macaroni,
And Count Vermicelli, his intimate crony ;
Both men of such *taste,* their opinions are taken
From ortalou down to a rasher of bacon,
     What makes Kitty Spicer, and the little Miss Sago,
To auctions and milliners' shops ev'ry day go ?
What makes them to vie with each other and quarrel
Which spends the most money for splendid apparel?
Why, *spirit*—to shew they have much better sense
Than their fathers, who raised it by shillings and pence.
What sends Peter Tewkesbury every night
To the play with such infinite joy and delight?
Why, Peter's a critic, with true attic salt,
Can damn the performers, can hiss and find fault,
And tell when we ought to express approbation
By thumping, and clapping, and vociferation ;
So he gains our attention, and all must admire
Young Tewkesbury's judgement, his *spirit,* and fire.
But Jack Dilettante despises the play'rs,
To concerts and musical parties repairs,
With benefit tickets his pockets he fills,
Like a mountebank doctor distributes his bills ;
And thus his importance and interest shows,
By conferring his favours wherever he goes ;
He's extremely polite both to me and my cousin,
For he often desires us to take off a dozen ;
He has taste, without doubt, and a delicate ear,
No vile oratorios ever could bear ;
But talks of the op'ras and his *Signiora,*
Cries *bravo, benissimo, bravo, encora !*
And oft is so kind as to thrust in a note,
While old Lady Cuckoo is straining her throat ;
Or little Miss Wren, who's an excellent singer,
Then he points to the notes, with a ring on his finger,
And shews her the crotchet, the quaver and bar,
All the time that she warbles and plays the guitar :

Yet I think, though she's at it from morning till noon,
Her queer little thingumbob's never in tune.

 Thank Heaven! of late, my dear mother, my face is
Not a little regarded at all public places;
For I ride in a chair, with my hands in a muff,
And have bought a silk coat, and embroider'd the cuff;
But the weather was cold, and the coat it was thin,
So the taylor advis'd me to line it with skin:
But what with my *Nivernois'* hat can compare,
Bag-wig, and lac'd ruffles, and black solitare?
And what can a man of true fashion denote,
Like an ell of good ribbon tied under the throat?
My buckles and box in exquisite taste,
The one is of paper, the other of paste:
And sure no *Camayeu* was ever yet seen
Like that which I purchas'd at Wicksted's machine:
My stockings, of silk, are just come from the hosier,
For to-night I'm to dance with the charming Miss Tozyer:
So I'd have them to know, when I go to the ball,
I shall shew as much *taste* as the best of them all:
For a man of great fashion was heard to declare
He never beheld so engaging an air,
And swears all the world must my judgment confess,
My *solididity, sense, understanding* in dress;
My manners so form'd, and my wig so well curl'd,
I look like a man *of the very first world:*
But my person and figure you'll best understand
From the picture I've sent, by an eminent hand:
Shew it young Lady Betty, by way of endearance,
And to give her a spice of my mien and appearance.
Excuse any more, I'm in haste to depart,
For a dance is the thing that I love at my heart,
So now, my dear mother, &c. &c. &c.
  Bath, 1766.   S—— B—N—R—D.

LETTER XI.

MR. SIMKIN B—N—R—D, TO LADY B—N—R—D, AT
—— HALL, NORTH.

A Description of the Ball, with an Episode on Beau Nash.

WHAT joy at the ball, what delights have I fouud,
By all the bright circle encompass'd around!
Each moment with transport my bosom felt warm,
For what, my dear mother, like beauty can charm?
The remembrance alone, while their praise I rehearse,
Gives life to my numbers, and strength to my verse:
Then allow for the rapture the Muses inspire,
Such themes call aloud for poetical fire.
I've read how the Goddesses meet all above,
And throng the immortal assemblies of Jove,
When join'd with the Graces fair Venus appears,
Ambrosial sweet odours perfume all the spheres;
But the Goddess of Love, and the Graces and all,
Must yield to the beauties I've seen at the ball;
For Jove never felt such a joy at his heart;
Such a heat as these charming, sweet creatures impart.
In short—there is something in very fine women,
When they meet altogether, that's quite overcoming.
    Then say, O ye Nymphs that inhabit the shades
Of *Pindus'* sweet banks, *Heliconian* Maids!
Celestial Muses, ye Powers divine,
O say, for your memory's better than mine,
What troops of fair virgins assembled around,
What squadrons of heroes for dancing renown'd, }
Were rous'd by the fiddles' harmonious sound.
What Goddess shall first be the theme of my song }
Whose name the clear Avon may murmur along, }
And echo repeat all the vallies among! }
Lady Tettaton's sister, Miss Fubby Fatarmin,
Was the first that presented her person so charming;
Than whom more engaging, more beautiful none, }
A Goddess herself among Goddesses shone. }
Excepting the lovely Miss Towzer alone, }
'Tis she that has long been the toast of the town,
Tho' all the world knows her complexion is brown:

If some people think that her mouth be too wide,
Miss Towzer has numberless beauties beside;
A countenance noble, with sweet, pouting lips,
And a delicate shape from her waste to her hips;
Besides a prodigious rough, black head of hair,
All frizzled and curl'd o'er her neck that is bare;
I've seen the sweet creature but once I confess,
But her air, and her manner, and pleasing address,
All made me feel something I ne'er can express.

    But lo! on a sudden what multitudes pour
From Cambrian mountains, from Indian shore;
Bright maidens, bright widows, and fortunate swains,
Who cultivate Liffy's sweet borders and plains,
And they who their flocks in fair Albion feed,
Rich flocks and rich herds (so the gods have decreed,)
Since they quitted the pleasanter banks of the Tweed.
Yet here no confusion, no tumult is known,
Fair Order and Beauty establish their throne;
For order, and beauty, and just regulation
Support all the works of this ample creation.
For this, in compassion to mortals below,
The gods, their peculiar favour to show,
Sent Hermes to Bath in the shape of a Beau:
That grandson of Atlas came down from above
To bless all the regions of pleasure and love;
To lead the fair nymph thro' the various maze,
Bright beauty to marshal his glory and praise;
To govern, improve, and adorn the gay scene,
By the Graces instructed, and Cyprian queen:
As when in a garden delightful and gay,
Where Flora is wont all her charms to display,
The sweet hyacinthus with pleasure we view
Contend with narcissus in delicate hue;
The gard'ner industrious trims out his border,
Puts each odorifeous plant in its order:
The myrtle he ranges, the rose and the lily,
With iris, and crocus, and daffa-down-dilly;
Sweet-peas and sweet oranges all he disposes
At once to regale both your eyes and your noses:
Long reign'd the great Nash, this omnipotent Lord,
Respected by youth, and by parents ador'd;
For him not enough at a ball to preside,
The unwary and beautiful nymph would he guide,

Oft tell her a tale, how the credulous maid
By man, by perfidious man, is betrayed;
Taught Charity's hand to relieve the distrest,
While tears have his tender compassion exprest:
But alas! he is gone, and the city can tell
How in years and in glory lamented he fell;
Him mourn'd all the Dryads on Claverton's mount;
Him Avon deplor'd, him the Nymph of the Fount,
The Crystalline streams.
Then perish his picture, his statue decay,
A tribute more lasting the Muses shall pay.
If true what philosophers all will assure us,
Who dissent from the doctrine of great Epicurus,
That the spirit's immortal; as poets allow,
If life's occupations are follow'd below;
In reward of his labour, his virtue and pains,
Indulg'd, as a token of Proserpine's favour,
To preside at her balls in a cream-coloured beaver.
Then peace to his ashes—our grief be supprest,
Since we find such a phœnix has sprung from his nest:
Kind Heaven has sent us another professor,
Who follows the steps of his great predecessor.

   But hark! now they strike the melodious string,
The vaulted roof echoes, the mansions all ring;
At the sound of the hautboy, the bass and fiddle,
Sir Boreas Blubber steps forth in the middle;
Like a holly-hock, noble, majestic, and tall,
Sir Boreas Blubber first opens the ball;
Sir Boreas, great in the minuet known,
Since the day that for dancing his talents were shown, }
Where the science is practis'd by gentlemen grown. }
For in every science, in every profession,
We make the best progress at years of discretion.
How he puts on his hat, with a smile on his face,
And delivers his hand with an exquisite grace!
How genteelly he offers Miss Carrot before us,
Miss Carrot Fitz-Oozer, a niece of Lord Porus!
How nimbly he paces, how active and light!
One never can judge of a man at first sight;
But as near as I guess, from the size of his calf,
He may weigh about twenty-three stone and a half.

Now why should I mention a hundred or more,
Who went the same circle as others before,
To a tune that they play'd us a hundred times o'er?
See little Bob Jerom, old Chrysostom's son,
With a chitterlin shirt and a buckle of stone,—
What a cropt head of hair the young parson has on!
Emerg'd from his grizzle, th' unfortunate prig
Seems as if he was hunting all night for his wig;
Not perfectly pleas'd with the coat on his back,
Tho' the coat's a good coat, but alas, it is black!
With envious eyes he is doom'd to behold
The Captain's red suit that's embroider'd with gold!
How seldom mankind are content with their lot!
Bob Jerom two very good livings has got;
Yet still he accuses his parents deceas'd
For making a man of such spirit a priest.
Not so Master Marmozet, sweet little boy,
Mrs. Danglecub's hope, her delight, and her joy :
His pigeon-wing'd head was not dress'd quite so soon,
For it took up a barber the whole afternoon;
His jacket's well lac'd, and the ladies protest
Master Marmozet dances as well as the best:
Yet some think the boy would be better at school;
But I hear Mr. Danglecub's not such fool
To send a poor thing, with a spirit so meek,
To be flogg'd by a tyrant for Latin and Greek ;
For why should a child of distinction and fashion
Lay a heap of such silly nonsensical trash in ?
She wonders that parents to Eton should send
Five hundred great boobies, their manners to mend,
When the master that left it, though no one objects
To his care of the boys in all other respects,
Was extremely remiss, for a sensible man,
In never contriving some elegant plan
For improving their persons, and showing them how
To hold up their heads, and to make a good bow,
When they've got such a charming long room for a ball,
Where the scholars might practise, and masters and all :
But, what is much worse, what no parent would choose,
He burnt all their ruffles, and cut off their queues :
So he quitted the school with the utmost disgrace,
And just such another's come into his place.

She says that her son will his fortune advance
By learning so early to fiddle and dance;
So she brings him to Bath, which I think is quite right,
For they do nothing else here from morning till night;
And this is a lesson all parents should know,
To train up a child in the way he should go:
For, as Solomon says, you may safely uphold
He ne'er will depart from the same when he's old.
No doubt she's a woman of fine understanding,
Her air and her presence there's something so grand in;
So wise and discreet; and to give her her due,
Dear mother, she's just such a woman as you.

But who is that bombasin lady so gay,
So profuse of her beauties in sable array;
How she rests on her heel, how she turns out her toe,
How she pulls down her stays, with her head up to shew
Her lily-white bosom that rivals the snow;
'Tis the widow Quicklackit, whose husband last week,
Poor Stephen, went suddenly forth in a pique,
And push'd off his boat for the *Stygian* creek:
Poor Stephen! he never return'd from the bourn,
But left the disconsolate widow to mourn:
Three times did she faint when she heard of the news;
Six days did she weep, and all comfort refuse;
But Stephen, no sorrows, no tears can recall;
So she hallows the seventh, and comes to the ball:
For music, sweet music has charms to controul,
And tune up each passion that ruffles the soul!
What things have I read, and what stories been told
Of feats that were done by musicians of old!
I've heard a whole city was built from the ground
By magical numbers and musical sound;
And here it can build a good house in the square,
Or raise up a church where the godly repair.
I saw, t'other day in *a thing call'd an Ode*,
As it lay in a snug little house on the road,
How Saul was restor'd, tho' his sorrow was sharp,
When David the *Bethlemite* play'd on the harp:
'Twas music that brought a man's wife from *Old Nick*,
And at Bath has the pow'r to recover the sick:
Thus a lady was cured t'other day.—But 'tis time
To seal up my letter, and finish my rhyme.

Bath, 1766.   S—— B——R——N——D.

D 2

LETTER XII.

MR. SIMKIN B—N—R—D, TO LADY B—N—R—D, AT
—— HALL, NORTH.

A Modern Head-dress, with a little polite Conversation.

WHAT base and unjust accusations we find
Arise from the malice and spleen of mankind!
One would hope, my dear mother, that scandal would
     spare
The tender, the helpless, and delicate fair;
But, alas, the sweet creatures all find it the case
That Bath is a very censorious place.
Would you think that a person I met since I came,
(I hope you'll excuse my concealing his name,)
A splenetic, ill-natur'd fellow, before
A room full of very good company, swore
That, in spite of appearance, 'twas very well known
Their hair and their faces were none of their own;
And thus, without wit, or the least provocation,
Began an impertinent, formal oration:
" Shall nature thus lavish her beauties in vain,
For art and nonsensical fashion to stain?
The fair Jezebella what art can adorn,
Whose cheeks are like roses that blush in the morn?
As bright were her locks as in heaven are seen
Presented for stars by the Egyptian queen:
But, alas! the sweet nymph they no longer must deck,
No more shall they flow o'er her ivory neck;
Those tresses which Venus might take as a favour,
Fall a victim at once to an outlandish shaver;
Her head has he robb'd with as little remorse
As a fox-hunter crops both his dogs and his horse:
A wretch that, so far from repenting his theft,
Makes a boast of tormenting the little that's left:
And first, at her porcupine head he begins
To fumble and poke with his irons and pins,
Then fires all his crackers with horrid grimace,
And puffs off his vile *Rocambole* breath in her face,
Discharging a steam that the devil would choke,
From paper, pomatum, from powder, and smoke.

The patient submits, and with due resignation
Prepares for her fate, the next operation.
When lo! on a sudden a monster appears,
A horrible monster to cover her ears;—
What sign of the Zodiac is it he bears?
Is it Taurus's tail, or the *tete de Mouton*,
Or the beard of the Goat that he dares to put on?
'Tis a wig *en vergette*, that from Paris was brought,
Un tète comme il faut, that the varlet has bought
Of a beggar, whose head he has shav'd for a groat:
Now, fix'd to her head, does he frizzle and dab it—
'Tis a foretop no more, 'tis the skin of a rabbit.—
'Tis a muff—'tis a thing, that by all is confest
Is in colour and shape like a chaffinch's nest.

"O cease, ye fair virgins, such pains to employ,
The beauties of nature with paint to destroy;
See Venus lament, see the Loves and the Graces
All pine at the injury done to your faces!
Ye have eyes, lips, and nose; but your heads are no more
Than a doll, that is plac'd at a milliner's door."

I'm ashamed to repeat what he said in the sequel,
Aspersions so cruel as nothing can equal!
I declare I am shock'd such a fellow should vex
And spread all these lies of the innocent sex;
For whom, while I live, I will make protestation,
I've the highest esteem, and profound veneration:
I never so strange an opinion will harbour,
That they buy all the hair they have got of a barber;
Nor ever believe that such beautiful creatures
Can have any delight in abusing their features:
One thing though I wonder at much, I confess, is
The appearance they make in their different dresses;
For indeed they look very much like apparitions
When they come in the morning to hear the musicians;
And some I am apt to mistake at first sight,
For the mothers of those I have seen over night.
It shocks me to see them look paler than ashes,
And as dead in the eye as the busto of Nash is,
Who the evening before were so blooming and plump;
I'm griev'd to the heart when I go to the Pump;
For I take every morning a sup at the water,
Just to hear what is passing, and see what they're a'ter:

For I'm told the discourses of persons refined
Are better than books for improving the mind.
But a great deal of judgment's required in the skimming
The polite conversation of sensible women;
For they come to the Pump, as before I was saying,
And talk, all at once, while the music is playing:—
" Your servant, Miss Fitchet—good morning, Miss Stote."
" My dear Lady Riggledum, how is your throat?
Your Ladyship knows that I sent you a scrawl,
Last night to attend at your Ladyship's call, }
But I hear that your Ladyship went to the ball."
" Oh, Fitchet—don't ask me—good heavens preserve—
I wish there was no such thing as a nerve;
Half dead all the night—I protest and declare—
My dear little Fitchet, who dresses your hair?— }
You'll come to the Rooms, all the world will be there.
Sir Toby Mac Negus is going to settle
His tea-drinking night with Sir Philip O'Kettle.
I hear that they both have appointed the same:
The majority think that Sir Philip's to blame; }
I hope they won't quarrel—they're both in a flame!
Sir Toby Mac Negus much spirit has got,
And Sir Philip O'Kettle is apt to be hot."
" Have you read the *Bath Guide*, that ridiculous Poem?
What a scurrilous author! does nobody know him?"
" Young Billy Penwaggle, and Simius Chatter,
Declare 't is an ill-natur'd, half-witted satire."
" You know I'm engag'd, my dear creature, with you
And Mrs. Pamtickle, this morning at loo;
Poor thing! though she hobbled last night to the ball,
To-day she's so lame that she hardly can crawl;
Major Lignum has trod on the first joint of her toe—
That thing they play'd last was a charming concerto;
I don't recollect to have heard it before,
The minuet's good, but the jig I adore; }
Pray speak to Sir Toby to cry out *encore*."
Dear mother, I think this is excellent fun,
But if all I must write, I should never have done, }
So myself I subscribe your most dutiful son,

Bath, 1766.   S—— B—N—R—D.

LETTER XIII.

MR. SIMKIN B—N—R—D, TO LADY B—N—R—D, AT —— HALL, NORTH.

A Public Breakfast; Motives for the same.—A List of the Company.—A tender Scene.—An unfortunate Incident.

WHAT blessings attend, my dear mother, all those
Who to crowds of admirers their persons expose!
Do the gods such a noble ambition inspire?
Or gods do we make of each ardent desire?
O generous passion! 'tis your's to afford
The splendid assembly, the plentiful board;
To thee do I owe such a breakfast this morn,
As I ne'er saw before since the hour I was born.
'Twas you made my Lord Ragamuffin come here,
Who they say has been lately created a Peer;
And to-day, with extreme complaisance and respect, ask'd
All the people at Bath to a general breakfast.
  You've heard of my Lady Bunbutter, no doubt,
How she loves an assembly, fandango, or rout;
No lady in London is half so expert
At a snug private party her friends to divert:
But they say that of late she's grown sick of the town,
And often to Bath condescends to come down.
Her Ladyship's favourite house is the *Bear;*
Her chariots and servants and horses are there.
My Lady declares that *retiring* is good:
As all with a separate maintenance should:
For when you have put out the conjugal fire,
'Tis time for all sensible folk to retire:
If Hymen no longer his fingers will scorch,
Little Cupid for others can whip in his torch,
So pert is he grown since the custom began
To be married and parted as soon as you can.
  Now my Lord had the honour of coming down post,
To pay his respects to so famous a toast;
In hopes he her Ladyship's favour might win,
By playing the part of a host at an inn.
I'm sure he's a person of great resolution,
Though delicate nerves and a weak constitution:
For he carried us all to a place 'cross the river,
And swore that the Rooms were too hot for his liver.

He said it would greatly our pleasure promote
If we all for Spring Gardens set out in a boat:
I never as yet could his reason explain,
Why we all sallied forth in the wind and the rain;
For sure such confusion was never yet known:—
Here a cap and a hat—there a cardinal blown
While his Lordship, embroider'd and powder'd all o'er,
Was bowing, and handing the ladies ashore.
How the Misses did huddle and scuddle and run,
One would think to be wet must be very good fun;
For by waggling their tails they all seem'd to take pains
To moisten their pinions like ducks when it rains:
And 'twas pretty to see how, like birds of a feather,
The people of quality flock'd all together;
All pressing, addressing, caressing and fond,
Just the same as those animals are in a pond.
You've read all their names in the news, I suppose,
But for fear you have not, take the list as it goes.—

> There was Lady Greasewrister,
> And Madam Van-Twister,
> Her Ladyship's sister.
> Lord Cram and Lord Vulter
> Sir Brandish O'Culter,
> With Marshall Carouzer,
> And old Lady Mouser,

And the great Hanoverian Baron Pansmouser:
Besides many others, who all in the rain went,
On purpose to honour this great entertainment.
The company made a most brilliant appearance,
And ate bread and butter with great perseverance:
All the chocolate too that my Lord set before 'em,
The ladies dispatched with the utmost decorum.
Soft musical numbers were heard all around,
The horns and the clarions, echoing, sound:
  Sweet were the strains as od'rous gales that blow
    O'er fragrant banks, where pinks and roses grow.
The Peer was quite ravish'd; while close to his side
Sat Lady Bunbutter, in beautiful pride!
Oft turning his eyes, he with rapture survey'd
All the powerful charms she so nobly display'd.
As when at the feast of the great Alexander,
Timotheus, the musical son of Thersander,
Breath'd heavenly measures;

The prince was in pain,
And could not contain,
While Thais was sitting beside him ;
But, before all his Peers,
Was for shaking the spheres,
Such goods the kind gods did provide him;—

Grew bolder and bolder,
And cock'd up his shoulder,
Like the son of great Jupiter Ammon ;
'Till, at length, quite opprest,
He sunk on her breast,
And lay there as dead as a salmon.

O had I a voice that was stronger than steel,
With twice fifty tongues to express what I feel,
And as many good mouths, yet I never could utter
All the speeches my Lord made to Lady Bunbutter!
So polite all the time, that he ne'er touch'd a bit,
While she ate up his rolls, and applauded his wit:
For they tell me that men of true taste, when they treat,
Should talk a great deal, but they never should eat :
And if that be the fashion, I never will give
Any grand entertainment as long as I live :
For I'm of opinion 'tis proper to cheer
The stomach and bowels, as well as the ear.
Nor me did the charming concerto of Abel
Regale like the breakfast I saw on the table.
I freely will own I the muffins preferr'd
To all the genteel conversation I heard,
E'en though I'd the honour of sitting between
My Lady Stuff-Damask and Peggy Moreen, ⎫
Who both flew to Bath in the *nightly* machine. ⎬
Cries Peggy, " This place is enchantingly pretty ; ⎭
We never can see such a thing in the City ;
You may spend all your life-time in Cateaton-street,
And never so civil a gentleman meet ;   [thro',
You may talk what you please, you may search London
You may go to Carlisle's, and to Almac's too ;
And I'll give you my head if you find such a host,
For coffee, tea, chocolate, butter, and toast :
How he welcomes at once all the world and his wife,
And how civil to folk he ne'er saw in his life!"

" These horns," cries my Lady, " so tickle one's ear,
" Lard, what would I give that Sir Simon was here!
To the next public breakfast Sir Simon shall go,
For I find here are folks one may venture to know ;
Sir Simon would gladly his Lordship attend,
And my Lord would be pleas'd with so cheerful a friend."

So when we had wasted more bread at a breakfast
Than the poor of the parish have eat for this week past,
I saw all at once a prodigious great throng
Come bustling, and rustling, and jostling along;
For his Lordship was pleas'd that the company now
To my Lady Bunbutter should curtsey and bow;
And my Lady was pleas'd too, and seem'd vastly proud
At once to receive all the thanks of a crowd :
And when, like Chaldeans, we all had adored
This beautiful image set up by my Lord,
Some few insignificant folk went away,
Just to follow th' employments and calls of the day ;
But those who knew better their time how to spend,
The fiddling and dancing all chose to attend.
Miss Clunch and Sir Toby perform'd a *cotillion,*
Just the same as our Susan and Bob the postillion ;
All the while her Mamma was expressing her joy
That her daughter the morning so well could employ.

Now why should the Muse, my dear mother, relate
The misfortunes that fall to the lot of the great ?
As homeward we came—'tis with sorrow you'll hear
What a dreadful disaster attended the Peer !
For whether some envious god had decreed
That a Naiad should long to ennoble the breed,
Or whether his Lordship was charm'd to behold
His face in the stream, like Narcissus of old :—
In handing old Lady Bumfidget and daughter,
This obsequious Lord tumbled into the water:
But a nymph of the flood brought him safe to the boat,
And I left all the ladies a-cleaning his coat.

Thus the feast was concluded, as far as I hear,
To the great satisfaction of all that were there.
O may he give breakfasts as long as he stays,
For I ne'er ate a better in all my born days.
In haste I conclude, &c. &c. &c.

Bath, 1766.   S—— B—N—R—D.

LETTER XIV.

MISS PRUDENCE B—N—R—D, TO LADY ELIZ. M—D—SS,
AT —— CASTLE, NORTH.

*Miss Prudence B-n-r-d informs Lady Betty that she has been
elected to Methodism by a Vision.*

HEARKEN, Lady Betty, hearken
    To the dismal news I tell ;
How your friends are all embarking
    For the fiery gulph of hell !

Brother Simkin's grown a rakehell,
    Cards and dances ev'ry day ;
Jenny laughs at tabernacle,
    Tabby Runt is gone astray.

Blessed I, tho' once rejected,
    Like a little wand'ring sheep,
Who this morning was elected
    By a vision in my sleep.

For I dream'd an apparition
    Came, like Roger, from above ;
Saying, by divine commission,
    I must fill you full of love.

Just with Roger's head of hair on,
    Roger's mouth and pious smile ;
Sweet, methinks, as beard of Aaron,
    Dropping down with holy oil.

I began to fall a-kicking,
    Panted, struggled, strove, in vain ;
When the spirit whipt so quick in,
    I was cur'd of all my pain.

First I thought it was the night-mare
    Lay so heavy on my breast ;
But I found new joy and light there,
    When with heav'nly love possest.

Come again then, apparition,
　　Finish what thou has begun ;
Roger, stay ! thou soul's physician,
　　I with thee my race will run.

Faith her chariot has appointed,
　　Now we're stretching for the goal ;
All the wheels with grace anointed,
　　Up to heav'n to drive my soul.

The Editor, for many reasons, begs to be excused giving the Public the sequel of this young Lady's letter ; but if the Reader will please to look into the Bishop of Exeter's book, entitled " The Enthusiasm of Methodists and Papists compared," he will find many instances (particularly of young people) who have been elected in the manner above.

LETTER XV.

MR. SIMKIN B—N—R—D TO LADY B—N—R—D, AT —— HALL, NORTH

Serious Reflections of Mr. B-n-r-d :—His Bill of Expenses :
—Distresses of the Family :—A Farewell to Bath.

ALAS, my dear mother, our evil and good
By few is distinguish'd, by few understood !
How oft are we doom'd to repent at the end,
The events that our pleasantest prospects attend !
As Solon declar'd, in the last scene alone
All the joys of our life, all our sorrows are known.
When first I came hither, for vapours and wind,
To cure all distempers, and study mankind,
How little I dream'd of the tempest behind !
I never once thought what a furious blast
What storms of distress would o'erwhelm me at last.
How wretched am I ! what a fine declamation
Might be made on the subject of my situation !
I'm a fable !—an instance ! and serve to dispense
An example to all men of spirit and sense,
To all men of fashion, and all men of wealth,
Who come to this place to recover their health :

For my means are so small, and my bills are so large,
I ne'er can come home 'till you send a discharge.
Let the Muse speak the cause, if a Muse yet remain
To supply me with rhymes, and express all my pain.

      Paid bells and musicians,
      Drugs, nurse, and physicians,
Balls, raffles, subscriptions, and chairs;
      Wigs, gowns, skins, and trimming,
      Good books for the women,
Plays, concerts, tea, negus, and prayers:

      Paid the following schemes,
      Of all who it seems,
Make charity bus'ness their care;—
      A gamester decay'd
      And a prudish old maid,
By gaiety brought to despair:

      A fiddler of note,
      Who for lace on his coat,
To his tailor was much in arrears;
      An author of merit,
      Who wrote with such spirit,
The pillory took off his ears.

A sum, my dear mother, far heavier yet,
Captain Cormorant won when I learn'd lansquenet
Two hundred I paid him, and five am in debt.
For the five I had nothing to do but to write,
For the Captain was very well-bred and polite,
And took, as he saw my expences were great,
My bond, to be paid on the Clodpole estate ;
And asks nothing more, while the money is lent,
Than interest paid him at twenty per cent.
But I'm shock'd to relate what distresses befal
Miss Jenny, my sister, and Tabby, and all :—
Miss Jenny, poor thing, from this Bath expedition,
Was in hopes very soon to have chang'd her condition;
But rumour has brought certain things to her ear,
Which I ne'er will believe, yet am sorry to hear ;
' That the Captain, her lover, her dear Romeo,
Was banish'd the army a great while ago:

That his friends and his foes he alike can betray,
And picks up a scandalous living by play.'
But if e'er I could think that the Captain had cheated,
Or my dear Cousin Jenny unworthily treated,
By all that is sacred I swear, for his pains,
I'd cudgel him first, and then blow out his brains,
For the man I abhor like the devil, dear mother,
Who one thing conceals, and professes another.
  O how shall we know the right way to pursue!
Do the ills of mankind from religion accrue?
Religion, designed to relieve all our care,
Has brought my poor sister to grief and despair:
Now she talks of damnation, and screws up her face,
Then prates about Roger, and spiritual grace;
Her senses, alas, seem at once gone astray—
No pen can describe it, no letter convey.
  But *the man without sin*, that Moravian Rabbi,
Has perfectly cured the chlorosis of Tabby;
And, if right I can judge, from her shape and her face,
She soon may produce him an infant of grace.
  Now they say that all people in our situation
Are very fine subjects for regeneration;
But I think, my dear mother, the best we can do
Is to pack up our all, and return back to you.

> Farewell, then, ye streams,
>   Ye poetical themes!
> Sweet fountains for curing the spleen!
>   I'm griev'd to the heart,
>   Without cash to depart
> And quit this adorable scene.

> Where gaming and grace
>   Each other embrace,
> Dissipation and piety meet,
>   May all who've a notion
>   Of cards or devotion,
> Make Bath their delightful retreat.

Bath, 1766.   S—— B—N—R—D·

EPILOGUE

TO THE SECOND EDITION

OF THE

NEW BATH GUIDE.

*Criticisms, and the Guide's Conversation with Three Ladies of
Piety, Learning, and Discretion.*

THERE are who complain that my verse is severe.
And what is still worse that my book is too dear :
The Ladies protest that I keep no decorum
In setting such patterns of folly before 'em :
Some cannot conceive what the Guide is about,
With names so unmeaning to make such a rout.
Lady Dorothy Scrawl would engage to bespeak
A hundred such things to be made in a week ;
Madam Shuffledumdoo, more provoking than that,
Has sold your poor Guide for two fish and a mat ;
A sweet medium paper, a book of fine size,
And a print that I thought would have suited her eyes.
And another good lady of delicate taste
Cries, " Fie ! Mr. Bookseller, bring me some paste ;
I'll close up this leaf, or my daughter will skim
The cream of that vile methodistical hymn :"—
Then stuck me down fast, so unfit was my page
To meet the chaste eyes of this virtuous age.
    Guide.—O spare me, good madam, it goes to my heart
With my sweet methodistical letter to part.
Away with your paste ! 'tis exceedingly hard
Thus to torture and cramp an unfortunate bard :
How my Muse will be shock'd, when she's just taking
        flight,
To find that her pinions are fastened so tight !

First Lady.—Why you know, beyond reason, and
          decency too,
Beyond all respect to religion that's due,
Your dirty satirical work you pursue.
I very well know whom you mean to affront
In your pictures of Prudence and Tabitha Runt.
    Guide.—Indeed, my good ladies, religion and virtue
Are things that I never design'd any hurt to.
All poets and painters, as Horace agrees,
May copy from nature what figures they please ;
Nor blame the poor poet or painter, if you
In verse or on canvass your likeness should view.
I hope you don't think I would write a lampoon,
I'd be hanged at the foot of Parnassus as soon.
    Second Lady.—Prithee don't talk to me of your Horace
          and Flaccus,
When you come, like an impudent wretch to attack us.
What's Parnassus to you? Take away but your rhyme,
And the strains of the bellman are full as sublime.
    Third Lady.—Dost think that such stuff as thou writ'st
          upon Tabby,
Will procure thee a busto in Westminster Abbey?
    Guide.—'Tis true on Parnassus I never did dream,
Nor e'er did I taste of sweet Helicon's stream ;
My share of the fountain I'll freely resign
To those who are better belov'd by the Nine :
Give bustos to poets of higher renown,
I ne'er was ambitious in marble to frown :
Give laurels to those from the god of the lyre
Who catch the bright spark of ethereal fire ;
Who skill'd every passion at will to impart,
Can play round the head while they steal to the heart ;
Who, taught by Apollo to guide the bold steed,
Know when to give force, when to temper his speed :
My nerves all forsake me, my voice he disdains,
When he rattles his pinions—no more hears the reins,
But thro' the bright ether sublimely he goes,
Nor earth, air, or ocean, or mountains oppose.
For me 'tis enough that my toil I pursue,
Like the bee drinking sweets that exhale from the dew,
Content if Melpomene joins to my lay
One tender soft strain of melodious Gray ;
Thrice happy in your approbation alone,
If the following ode for my hymn can atone.

A LETTER

To Miss Jenny W—d—r, at Bath, from Lady Eliz.
M—d—ss, her Friend in the Country;

A Young Lady of neither Fashion, Taste, nor Spirit.

Oft I've invok'd the Aonian quire,
  And Phœbus oft in vain,
Like thee, my friend, to tune my lyre,
  Like thee to raise my strain:

And when, of late, I sought their aid
  The flow'ry bank beside,
Methought, along the silent glade,
  I heard a voice that cry'd—

" Mistaken maid! why idly waste
  Your hours in fruitless toil?
You ne'er the hallow'd brook can taste,
  Or tread poetic soil.

" For since your friend pursues the path
  Where wit and pleasure reigns,
With her has fled each Muse to Bath,
  From these neglected plains.

" There many a bard's inspir'd with song,
  With epigram and ode;
And *one* the meanest of the throng,
  Takes satire's thorny road.

" For him Bath's injur'd Genius now
  The hemlock juice prepares,
And deadly nightshade o'er his brow
  For laurel wreaths he wears.

" Him, like the Thracian bard, shall curse
  Each nymph, each angry dame;
Though far inferior be his verse,
  His hapless fate the same.

" Torn be the wretch, whose impious strains
  Profaned their beauty's pride,
No Muse to gather his remains
  That flow down Avon's tide;

" But him shall many a drone pursue
  That hums around the stream;
Him frantic priests, an insect crew
  That crowd LIGHT's heav'nly beam.

" Then, lest his destiny you share,
    Rash nymph, thy strains give o'er !
Be warn'd by me, of rhyme beware !"
    The voice was heard no more.

Yet though I cease my artless lay,
    Nor longer court the Nine,
This faithful tribute will I pay
    At friendship's sacred shrine.

Here will I offer incense sweet,
    Here light the hallow'd fires :
And oh ! with kind acceptance meet
    What true regard inspires.

Nor let my friendly verse offend
    That poor deluded maid,*
Whose *faith* I ne'er can comprehend,
    Or *grace* in dreams convey'd.

May no such *grace* my thoughts employ,
    Nor I with envy view
Those scenes of dissipated joy
    So well describ'd by you !

Think not a parent's harsh decrees
    From me those scenes withhold ;
His soft request can ne'er displease,
    Who ne'er my joys controul'd.

But pining years opprest with grief
    My tender care demand ;
The bed of sickness asks relief
    From my supporting hand.

Well do I know how sorrow preys,
    E'er since the hour that gave
The partner of his happier days
    To seek the silent grave.

In that sad hour my lips she prest,
    Bedew'd with many a tear ;
And " take," she cried, " this last bequest,
    A dying mother's prayer.

" O let the maxims I convey
    Sink deep into thy breast,
When I no more direct thy way,
    Retired to endless rest.

* MISS PRUDENCE B—N—DR—HD

" Look on thy aged father's woe!
    'Tis thine to soothe his pain:
With GRACE like this, religion shew,
    And thus her cause maintain.

" Nor is't enough that grace displays,
    Or faith her light divine;
In all thy works, in all thy ways,
    Let heav'nly virtue shine:

" O! may the fountain of all truth
    Each perfect gift impart,
With innocence protect thy youth,
    With hope support thy heart!

" So may'st thou learn thyself to know,
    Of all extremes beware,
Nor find in age thy cup o'erflow
    With shame, remorse, and care:

" Then shall no madmen LIGHT reveal,
    No visionary priest,
With falsehood, ignorance, and zeal,
    Torment thy peaceful breast:

" Then shall no fears thy soul distress,
    Religion's doubts shall cease:
Her ways are ways of pleasantness,
    And all her paths are peace."

Such were the truths ere lost in death
    Her parting voice convey'd;
Such may I keep till latest breath,
    Thou dear lamented shade!

What though no Muse will deign, my friend,
    My homely joys to tell;
Though Fashion ne'er will condescend
    To seek this humble cell;

Yet freedom, peace, and mind serene,
    Which modish life disdains,
(Perpetual sweets!) enrich the scene
    Where conscious virtue reigns.

Blest scenes! such unrepented joys,
    Such true delights ye give,
Remote from fashion, vice, and noise,
    Contented let me live.

                ELIZ. MODELESS.

*The Conversation continued—The Ladies' Receipt for a
      Novel—The Ghost of Mr. Quin.*

    Guide.—Now I hope that this letter from young Lady
       Betty,
Will be reckon'd exceedingly decent and pretty:
That you, my good ladies, who ne'er could endure
A hymn so *ineffably vile and impure,*
My indelicate Muse will no longer *bewail,*
Since a sweet little moral is pinn'd to her tail!
If not, as so kindly I'm tutor'd by you,
Pray tell a poor Poet what's proper to do.
    First Lady.—Why if thou must write, thou had'st better
       compose
Some *novels,* or elegant letters in prose:
Take a subject that's grave, with a moral that's good,
Throw in all the temptations that virtue withstood,
In epistles like Pamela's chaste and devout—
A book that *my family's never without.*
    Second Lady.—O pray let your hero be handsome and
       young,
Taste, wit, and fine sentiment flow from his tongue;
His delicate feelings be sure to improve
With passion, with tender soft rapture, and love.
    Third Lady.—Add some incidents too, which I like
       above measure,
Such as those *which I've heard* are esteem'd as a treasure
In a book that's intitled—*The Woman of Pleasure.*
Mix well, and you'll find 'twill a *novel* produce
Fit for modest young ladies—so keep it for use.
    Guide.—Damnation!—*(aside.)*—Well, ladies, I'll do
       what I can,
And ye'll bind it, I hope, with your *Duty of Man.*
    Guide mutters.—*Take a subject that's grave with a moral*
       that's good;—
Thus musing, I wander'd in splenetic mood
Where the languid old Cam rolls his willowy flood

When lo! beneath a poplar's glimm'ring shade,
Along the stream where trembling oziers play'd,
What time the bat low-flitting skims the ground,
When beetles buz, when gnats are felt around,
And hoarser frogs their am'rous descant sound;—
Sweet scenes! that heav'nly contemplation give,
And oft in musical description live!—
When now the moon's refulgent rays begin
O'er twilight groves to spread their mantle thin,
Sudden arose the awful form of Quin:
A form that bigger than the life appear'd,
And head like Patagonian Hero rear'd.
Aghast I stood! when lo! with mild command
And looks of courtesy, he wav'd his hand,
Me to th' embowering grove's dark path convey'd,
And thus began the venerable shade:—
" Forth from Elysium's blest abodes I come,
Regions of joy, where Fate has fix'd my doom.
Look on my face—I well remember thine;
Thou knew'st me too, when erst, in life's decline,
At Bath I dwelt—there late reposed mine age,
And unrepining left this mortal stage:
Yet do those scenes, once conscious of delight,
Rejoice my social ghost! there oft by night
I hold my way:
And from the mullet, and the sav'ry jole
Catch fragrant fumes, that still regale my soul!
Sweet Bath, which thou these dreary banks along
Oft mak'st the subject of thy wayward song——"
    Guide.—O spare me, blest spirit——
    Ghost.—Quit thy vain fears; I come not to accuse
The motley labours of thy mirthful Muse;
For well, I ween, if rightly understood,
Thy themes are pleasant, and thy moral good.
Oft have I read the laughter-moving phrase
And splayfoot measures of thy Simkin's lays,
Nor aught *indecent or obscene* I find,
That virtue wounds, or taints the virgin's mind:
Beware of that—O! why should I describe
What ills await the caitiff *scribbling tribe?*
First see the mob who *novels lewd* dispense,
The bane of virtue, modesty, and sense:
Next that infernal crew, detractors base,
Who pen *lampoons,* true satire's foul disgrace:

Nor less the punishment in realms below
For those who *praise unmerited* bestow,
Those pimps in science, who, with dulness bold,
The sacred Muses prostitute for gold;
Those too whom zeal to pious wrath inclines,
Pedantic, proud, polemical divines:
Bad Critics last, whom Rhadamanth severe
Chastises first, then condescends to hear:
All, all in fiery Phlegethon must stay,
Till gall, and ink, and dirt of scribbling day, }
In purifying flames are purg'd away.

   Guide.—O trust me, blest spirit, I ne'er would offend
One innocent virgin, one virtuous friend:
From nature alone are my characters drawn,
From *little* Bob Jerom to Bishops in lawn:
Sir Boreas Blubber, and such stupid faces,
Are at London, at Bath, and all public places;
And if to Newmarket I chance to repair,
'Tis odds but I see Captain Cormorant there:
But he who his cash on physicians bestows,
Meets a *tight little Doctor* wherever he goes.

   Ghost.—'Tis true such insects as thy tale has shown
Breathe not the atmosphere of Bath alone,
Though there, in gaiety's meridian ray,
Vain fools, like flies, their gaudy wings display;
Awhile they flutter, but their sunshine past,
Their fate, like Simkin, they lament at last.
Worse ills succeed; oft superstition's gloom—
Sheds baneful influence o'er their youthful bloom—
Such Heav'n avert from fair Britannia's plains,
To realms were bigotry and slavery reigns!
No more of that. But stay, thou tim'rous bard,
Claim not the WINES of Bath thy just regard?
Where oft, I ween, the brewer's chaldron flows
With elder's mawkish juice, and puck'ring sloes,
Cyder and hot Geneva they combine,
Then call the fatal composition WINE.
By Cerberus I swear, not those vile crews,
Who vend their pois'nous med'cines by the news,
For means of death, air, earth and seas explore,
Have sent such numbers to the *Stygian* shore:
Shun thou such base potations; oft I've thought
My span was shorten'd by the noxious draught.—

But, soft, my friend !—is this the soil, the clime,
That teaches Granta's tuneful sons to rhyme ?
On me unsavoury vapours seem to fix,
Worse than Cocytus or the pools of Styx ;
Inspired by fogs of this slow-winding Cam,
O say, does —— presume thy strains to damn ?
Heed not that miscreant's tongue ; pursue thy ways,
Regardless of his censure or his praise.

    Guide.—But if any old lady, knight, priest, or physician,
Should condemn me for printing a second edition :
If good Madam Squintum my work should abuse,
May I venture to give her a smack of my Muse ?

    Ghost.—By all manner of means : if thou find'st that the case,
Tho' she cant, whine, and pray, never mind her grimace
Take the mask from her d—n'd hypocritical face.

    Guide.—Come on, then, ye Muses, I'll laugh down my day,
In spite of them all will I carol my lay ;
But perish my voice, and untun'd be my lyre,
If my verse one indelicate thought should inspire :
Ye angels ! who watch o'er the slumbering fair,
Protect their sweet dreams, make their virtue your care !
Bear witness yon moon, the chaste empress of night !
Yon stars that diffuse the pure heavenly light !
How oft have I mourn'd that such blame should accrue
From one wicked letter of pious Miss Prue !
May this lazy stream, who to Granta bestows
Philosophical slumbers, and learned repose,
To Granta, sweet Granta where studious of ease
Seven years did I sleep, and then lost my* degrees,
May this drowsy current (as oft as he's wont)
O'erflow all my hay, may my dogs never hunt,
May those ills to torment me, those curses conspire,
Which so oft plague and crush an unfortunate 'Squire,
Some May'r to cajole me, some lawyer to chowse,
For a seven months' seat in the parliament-house,
There to finish my nap, for the good of the nation,
'Wake—Frank—and be thank'd by the whole corporation.
Then a poor tenant come. when my cash is all spent,
With a bag-full of *tax-bills* to pay me his rent ;

* Vide University Register, Proctor's Books, &c.

And O! may some demon, these plagues to complete,
Give me *taste* to *improve* an old family seat,
By *lawning* an hundred good acres of wheat.
Such ills be my portion, and others much worse,
If slander or calumny poison my verse,
If ever my well-behav'd Muse shall appear
Indecently droll, unpolitely severe.

Good ladies, uncensur'd, Bath's pleasures pursue,
May the springs of old Bladud your graces renew.
I never shall mingle with gall the pure stream,
But make your examples and virtues my theme:
Nor fear, ye sweet virgins, that aught I shall speak,
To call the chaste blush o'er your innocent cheek.
O frown not, if haply your poet once more,
Should seek the delightful *Avonian* shore,
Where oft he the winter's dull season beguiles,
Drinks health, life, and joy from your heavenly smiles.

TO THE GHOST.

For thee, who to visit these regions of spleen,
Deign'st to quit the sweet vales of perpetual green,
Forsake, happy Shade, this *Bœotian* air,
Fly hence—to *Elysium's* pure ether repair,
Rowe, Dryden, and Otway—thy Shakspeare is there:
There Thomson, poor Thomson, ingenious bard,
Shall equal thy friendship, thy kindness reward,
Thy praise in mellifluous numbers prolong,
Who cherish'd his Muse and gave life to his song.
And O may thy genius, blest spirit, impart
To me the same virtues that glow'd in thy heart,
To me, with thy talents convivial, give
The art to enjoy the short time I shall live ;
Give manly, give rational mirth to my soul,
O'er the social sweet joys of the full-flowing bowl!
So ne'er may vile scribblers thy memory stain,
Thy forcible wit may no blockheads profane,
Thy faults be forgotten, thy virtues remain.
Farewell! may the turf where thy cold reliques rest,
Bear herbs, odoriferous herbs, o'er thy breast,
Their heads, *thyme*, and *sage*, and *pot-marjoram* wave,
And fat be the gander that feeds on thy grave.

THE END.